IT'S TIME TO LEARN ABOUT BOA CONSTRICTORS

It's Time to Learn about Boa CONSTRICTORS

Walter the Educator

Silent King Books
A WhichHead Entertainment Imprint

Copyright © 2025 by Walter the Educator

All rights reserved. No part of this book may be reproduced in any manner whatsoever without written per- mission except in the case of brief quotations embodied in critical articles and reviews.

First Printing, 2024

Disclaimer

This book is a literary work; the story is not about specific persons, locations, situations, and/or circumstances unless mentioned in a historical context. Any resemblance to real persons, locations, situations, and/or circumstances is coincidental. This book is for entertainment and informational purposes only. The author and publisher offer this information without warranties expressed or implied. No matter the grounds, neither the author nor the publisher will be accountable for any losses, injuries, or other damages caused by the reader's use of this book. The use of this book acknowledges an understanding and acceptance of this disclaimer.

It's Time to Learn about Boa CONSTRICTORS is a collectible early learning book by Walter the Educator suitable for all ages belonging to Walter the Educator's Time to Eat Book Series. Collect more books at WaltertheEducator.com

USE THE EXTRA SPACE TO TAKE NOTES AND DOCUMENT YOUR MEMORIES

BOA CONSTRICTORS

Deep in the jungle, dark and wide,

It's Time to Learn about
Boa Constrictors

A sneaky snake likes to hide.

With patterned scales both smooth and long,

The boa slithers, swift and strong.

It has no legs, it has no feet,

But moves so fast, now isn't that neat?

With muscles tight, it twists and glides,

Through trees and grass, it smoothly slides.

The boa doesn't chase its prey,

It waits so still throughout the day.

Then when a mouse or bird comes near,

The boa strikes, it's quick and clear!

It doesn't bite to eat its food,

It wraps around, so strong and shrewd.

A gentle squeeze, a hug so tight,

Until the meal gives up the fight.

It's Time to Learn about
Boa Constrictors

Then, with a mouth so big and wide,

The boa swallows all inside!

No need to chew, just gulp it down,

And rest a while on the ground.

After eating, full and slow,

The boa finds a place to go.

It lies in shade, so still, so neat,

It might not eat again for weeks!

Boa CONSTRICTORSs climb with ease,

Through jungle vines and tall, strong trees.

Their tails can grip, their bodies bend,

They twist and turn, they find their friends.

Some boas live where it is dry,

In rocky lands beneath the sky.

In deserts, forests, trees so tall,

It's Time to Learn about
Boa Constrictors

Boas can live just about all!

They grow so big, so long, so wide,

Some stretch out ten feet, or more beside!

But don't you fear, they won't chase you,

They only hunt for what they chew.

So if you see one, don't feel fear,

Just watch it move and stay right here.

The boa's strong, but it won't bite,

It's Time to Learn about
Boa Constrictors

A secret hunter of the night!

ABOUT THE CREATOR

Walter the Educator is one of the pseudonyms for Walter Anderson. Formally educated in Chemistry, Business, and Education, he is an educator, an author, a diverse entrepreneur, and he is the son of a disabled war veteran. "Walter the Educator" shares his time between educating and creating. He holds interests and owns several creative projects that entertain, enlighten, enhance, and educate, hoping to inspire and motivate you. Follow, find new works, and stay up to date with Walter the Educator™

at WaltertheEducator.com

www.ingramcontent.com/pod-product-compliance
Lightning Source LLC
LaVergne TN
LVHW051919060526
838201LV00060B/4076